THE INVISIBLE ONE

By S. Payne

DEDICATION

To every woman who ever felt unseen.
To every child who learned fear too young.
To every soul who walked through fire and did not
know faith was already carrying them.
This is for you.

ACKNOWLEDGMENTS

To God — who found me in darkness and carried me when I had nothing left.

To my husband — who puts up with me and loves me just the way I am.

To my children and grandchildren — my heartbeats, my purpose.

To my sister Katy — the quiet to my loud, the faith to my fire.

To her family — who became mine.

To every soul reading this — thank you.

TABLE OF CONTENTS

CHAPTER 1 - The Invisible Beginning

"Do not despise these small beginnings, for the Lord rejoices to see the work begin" Zech 4:10

My parents wanted children badly. They were already filling out adoption paperwork when the surprise came—they were expecting me.

While my mom was pregnant, she used to tell the story of one strange evening when her entire belly flipped. At the time, she did not understand what it meant. Later, she would learn that was the moment I turned and dislocated my hips—something she would not discover until six months after I was born.

What was clear from the start was that the umbilical cord had wrapped around my neck—not once, but twice.

The devil tried to take me out then.

My mother labored for twenty-two long hours before doctors finally decided to take me by C-section. I came into this world already fighting—already refusing to let go of breath, already clinging to life.

Six months later, the truth about my hips finally surfaced. I was placed in casts, locked into a metal bar that ran from one leg to the other. While other babies learned to crawl freely, my body learned restraint before it learned movement. My bones were being shaped by force, by correction, by survival.

Soon after, my younger sister Penny was born—exactly one year and a half after me, to the day.
I was born February 4, 1969.
She was born August 4, 1970.

There are pictures somewhere—proof that even then, I was waiting. In them, I'm standing by the door, small and stiff, watching for her to come home. Already positioned as the watcher. The protector. The one looking outward instead of inward.

I did not know it then, but that posture—waiting, watching, bracing—would follow me for the rest of my life.

I must have been three or four years old when the next moment changed everything.

I was playing on the basement steps. There was no railing—no protection at all—and I misjudged where one step ended and the next began. I did not know yet that my depth perception was off. I did not know the world disappeared on one side.

I stepped where I thought solid ground would be.

Instead, I fell.

I went headfirst, my skull slamming into the concrete floor. The sound echoed and then everything went dark. I did not cry. I did not scream. I did not move.

I was out cold.

My parents panicked. They grabbed me in a rush so frantic they almost forgot Penny. And just like that, we were gone—off to the hospital, fear driving faster than reason.

I stayed knocked out for days.

When I finally came to, the room felt strange—too bright, too quiet. A doctor stood near my bed and asked me a question that confused me.

"Do you wear glasses?"

I nodded and said yes.

In my little mind, I thought he meant sunglasses.

That is when they discovered the truth.

I was blind in my right eye.

I always had been.

The fall was not because I was careless. It was not because I was wild or reckless. It was because I could not tell where the step ended. The edge simply disappeared.

And just like that, blindness joined the list of things that would shape my life—another silent burden, another invisible difference I would learn to hide long before I learned to understand it.

I entered this world already fighting for breath.
And before I ever learned how to live,
I learned how to survive.

CHAPTER 2 - Broken Before I Could Speak

"For the mountains may depart and the hills be removed, but my steadfast love shall not depart from you, and my covenant of peace shall not be removed, says the Lord, who has compassion on you" Isaiah 54:10

If Chapter 1 was about how I entered the world broken, then this chapter is about how the world continued breaking me—slowly, quietly, and repeatedly—before I ever learned how to name what was happening.

There is a kind of pain that becomes the air you breathe as a child. It does not announce itself. It does not always scream. It just exists—constant and familiar—until you do not even recognize it as pain anymore.

That was my normal.

I never saw my mother and father hug. I never saw them kiss. But I remember the holes punched into the paneling. I remember the yelling, the crying, the way fear lived in the walls.

I remember being hidden in the car at the drive-in movies, tucked away like something that needed protecting from the world—or maybe from him. I remember my father stealing from department stores, and I remember him washing windows high up on ladders, balancing danger with carelessness like it was nothing.

My mother loved us back then. I know she did. She tried in the ways she knew how. But my father— my father only seemed to love me.

I was Daddy's little girl.

And my poor baby sister, Penny, bore the weight of that imbalance.

My father loved football. He was always made to watch it in the basement, separated from the rest of the house like a ticking bomb contained behind a door. Penny and I played down there too, trying to stay out of his way, trying to be quiet, trying to disappear.

Sometimes Penny would get too close.

That is when it would happen.

The roll of his tongue.

The sound that meant run.

We would scatter, instinct kicking in before thought. But sometimes Penny wasn't fast enough. He would chase her, grab her, pull her hair, hit her. And I would run after him—crying, begging, pleading for him to stop. I remember my voice breaking before my heart did, screaming words that never seemed to reach him.

It always got worse before it stopped.

Until one day, my mother had enough.

I do not remember the exact words she used, but I remember the finality of it. She told him to leave. And this time, she meant it.

I was sitting on my twin bed, practicing how to tie a bow with a ribbon, when Uncle Joey came to get him. I remember the stillness after—the quiet that did not feel peaceful yet, just unfamiliar.

That was the last time we saw my father for a long while.

Fear did not leave with him at once. It lingered, unsure where to go. Trauma does not pack its bags neatly. It settles into the nervous system, into memory, into the way a child learns to watch instead of relax.

I learned early that love could be uneven.
That protection could come too late.
That silence could be louder than screams.

And yet—even then—something inside me was forming.

I did not have words for trauma yet, but I had the symptoms.

The stomachaches.

The constant alertness.
The inability to rest.
The instinct to protect others before myself.

I was learning fear.
I was learning survival.

And without knowing it, I was learning endurance.

I would need it.

Because this was only the beginning.

CHAPTER 3 - What Lived in the House

"Have I not commanded you? Be strong and courageous. Do not be afraid; do not be discouraged, for the Lord your God will be with you wherever you go." Joshua 1:9

After my father left, everything changed.

My mother had never worked while he lived with us. Suddenly, she was on her own—raising two children, one with medical issues, trying to hold together a life that had already been cracked in too many places. I do not know how she did it. I really do not. Looking back now, I can only guess that my grandmother helped more than I ever realized.

Grandma was around a lot then—especially before and after school. We were still young, and Mom had to work. Mornings belonged to Grandma.

She had a way of waking us up that I absolutely hated.

She would sneak into our room and tickle our feet until we jerked awake, laughing and yelling, half-asleep and already annoyed. I hated it. Every single time. But that was her love—playful, invasive, impossible to ignore.

That woman was always there.

Grandma also loved tarot cards and tea leaves. Reading them was not something she hid—it was just part of life. She taught me at a young age, like it was no different than teaching a child how to read or count. Cards spread across the table. Cups turned upside down. Symbols explained like facts.

This was normal in our house.

My mother dealt with the spirits.

And there were spirits in that house.

Some of them were terrifying.

Things moved—chairs, tables—without anyone touching them. Doors creaked open on their own. You could feel when something was not right, like the air itself shifted. Later, when we were older, Penny had a full-blown confrontation in the kitchen. Cabinets flew open. Drawers slammed out. Everything inside them came crashing down onto the floor.

We were not imagining it.

Strange things happened in that house—things we did not question because we did not know to question them. There were séances. Astral planning. Tarot readings. Channeling. Spells. Binding rituals. Full moons meant chaos—voices, energy, restlessness that made sleep almost impossible.

Later, we would learn what to call it.

We were Wiccan.

At the time, it did not feel strange—it felt like belonging. Like answers. Like control in a world that had taken so much from us already. When your life feels unsafe, you reach for anything that promises understanding or power.

I thank God now for the line I never crossed.
I never killed an animal.

But I saw enough. I felt enough. And those doors, once opened, are not easily shut.

That house held more than memories.
It held fear.
It held trauma.
It held things that watched back.

I did not know it then, but I was learning another dangerous lesson:

That darkness does not always announce itself as evil.
Sometimes it introduces itself as comfort.
Sometimes it feels like home.

CHAPTER 4 - School Taught me What Home Did Not

"Do not seek revenge or bear a grudge against anyone among your people, but love your neighbor as yourself. I am the Lord." Leviticus 19:18

School was supposed to be the safe place. That is what adults said, anyway. It had rules, schedules, bells that told you where to be and when. In theory, it was orderly and predictable. A place where effort mattered and fairness existed. In practice, it was where I learned that being different comes with a price.

I did not see the world the way other kids did— literally. Depth perception was not my friend. My eyes did not cooperate the way they were supposed to, and no amount of squinting or trying harder fixed that. Letters blurred. Chalkboards mocked me. Distance lied to me.

I learned quickly that confusion looks a lot like stupidity if you do not have the language to explain it. I went to school with a patch on my right eye, following the doctors' belief that it might help my damaged eye recover some vision. It did not work. What it did do was make me different—and that became an invitation for bullying.

Teachers thought I was not paying attention. Kids thought I was weird. And I thought it was my fault. Classrooms were loud with judgment, whispers, kids who noticed I missed things and decided that was entertaining. I was the easy target—the one who did not catch what was written, who answered wrong, who tilted her head just enough for people to notice.

They learned my weakness before I learned how to protect it. I learned how to shrink in public, how to make myself smaller without physically disappearing, and how to pretend I did not care while cataloging every insult for later.

There is a special kind of loneliness that comes from being surrounded by people and still feeling completely alone. You start to believe that if no one is stepping in, maybe this is just what you deserve. So, I adapted. I learned when to laugh at myself before someone else could. I learned how to be "tough." I learned how to be quick with my mouth and quicker with my exits.

When school stopped feeling survivable, I started looking for other places that did.

CHAPTER 5 - Where the Streets Felt Kinder

"For our struggle is not against flesh and blood, but against the rulers, against the authorities, against the powers of this dark world and against the spiritual forces of evil in the heavenly realms."
Ephesians 6:12

By fourth grade, I understood something very clearly: If I stayed where I was supposed to be, I would get hurt. If I left, I might survive, being seen was too risky. That realization did not feel rebellious; it felt practical. It felt like self-preservation. I did not know yet where I was going; I just knew I could not stay.

So, I started cutting class. I would leave the house like I was going to school—backpack on, face straight, playing the part. But instead of turning toward the building that held lockers and cruelty, I went the other way. I found my way to the avenue in Kensington.

That's where I met the other kids like me.

Kids who did not fit in.
Kids who did not belong anywhere else.
Kids who already knew how to disappear.

We walked the railroad tracks like they were ours, balancing on rusted steel, daring each other not to fall. We smoked pot because it slowed everything down—my thoughts, my fear, the constant buzzing inside my chest. For the first time, my body could breathe.

We hopped on trains, on and off, laughing like nothing bad could ever touch us while we were moving. Motion felt like freedom. As long as I did not stay still, nothing could catch me. Sometimes, I would sit on a stoop and watch the world blur. Faces melted into shapes, movement without detail. People assume blindness is darkness. It is not. It is distortion. It is knowing something is there but never being able to grasp it fully. That is how my life felt — always reaching, always missing. there was relief in disappearing for a while.

I was not trying to be bad. I was trying to breathe. The streets did not judge me. They did not patch my eyes. They did not lock me in closets. The streets did not pretend to care and then hurt me anyway. They let me get away. No one asked questions I could not answer. No one demanded things I could not give. No one punished me for being broken. On the streets, being broken was normal.

I did not understand it then, but I was already learning a dangerous lesson:

That escape feels like safety. That numbness feels like peace. That belonging—even in the wrong places—feels better than rejection everywhere else.

I was not looking to be bad. I was not looking to rebel. I was looking for somewhere that did not hurt. And for a while, the streets felt like mercy, but mercy borrowed from the streets always comes with a cost; I just had not paid it yet.

CHAPTER 6 - When Belonging Comes with a Price

"Even there Your hand will guide me, Your right hand will hold me fast." — Psalm 139:10

Belonging is a dangerous thing when you have gone your whole life without it. Once I found a place where I was not questioned, I clung to it like oxygen. The streets did not love me, but they did not reject me either. And when you have been rejected everywhere else, neutrality feels like affection.

I started staying gone longer. One skipped class turned into whole days. Days turned into nights. I learned how to disappear without anyone noticing—which, looking back, is its own kind of tragedy. No truancy officer came looking. No teacher asked where I had been. No one pulled me aside and said, Are you okay?

So, I answered that question myself. I told myself I was fine.

We had routines, certain corners, certain tracks, certain places you did not go unless you knew who controlled them. I watched people read danger like a second language—the way their shoulders stiffened, the way their voices dropped. I could not always see the warning signs, so I learned to feel them. Vibes mattered more than vision. If the air felt wrong, it was wrong. I trusted my gut long before I trusted my eyes.

Drugs were not the point at first. Escape was. Being quiet inside was addictive. The noise in my head—the fear, the memories, the constant vigilance—finally dimmed. For the first time, I was not bracing for the next hit, the next insult, the next humiliation.

But numbness lies.

It whispers that you are safe when you are actually slipping. It convinces you that control is yours when it is already gone. I did not wake up one day and decide to spiral. I drifted—slow enough that it felt normal.

There were moments of kindness, and those were the most dangerous. Older kids who shared food. Strangers who said I was smart, funny, fearless. They did not know the little girl behind my eyes who still wanted someone to sit next to her and mean it.

And then there were moments that cracked the illusion.

Fights that erupted without warning. Friends turning on each other over nothing. The first time I realized someone I cared about had disappeared for good—not grounded, not moved away, but gone. No goodbye. No explanation. Just absence.

Her name was Mary. I would later learn she had overdosed.

That is when I learned the truth: Belonging that is not rooted in love will always demand payment. Sometimes the cost was safety. Sometimes dignity. Sometimes innocence.

I started doing things I swore I would not do—not because I wanted to, but because saying no felt like risking exile. And exile felt worse than anything. Fear of being alone will make you compromise pieces of yourself you do not know how to get back.

At night, when everything finally went quiet, the noise returned. That is when something inside me would stir—steady, persistent, impossible to drown out completely. I did not know what it was. I thought it was guilt. Or instinct. Or weakness.

Now I know it was God.

I did not understand then that He does not shout over chaos. He waits patiently for you to get tired of running. He lets you choose, even when your choices break His heart.

I was choosing survival the only way I knew how. But survival without direction is just a slower kind of destruction. By the time I realized I was losing myself, I did not know how to stop. The streets that once felt like freedom started to feel like a trap. The belonging I fought so hard for tightened around my chest.

And still—I stayed.

Because leaving meant facing everything I had been avoiding. And I was not ready to look at my life without numbing it first. I did not know then that this chapter of my life was not punishment.

It was preparation.

CHAPTER 7 - The Invitation That Changed Everything

"The temptations in your life are no different from what others experience. And God is faithful. He will not allow the temptation to be more than you can stand." 1 Cor. 10:13

When there was nothing to distract me, memories crept in. The classrooms where I could not see. The lockers. The laughters. The feeling of being small and trapped and powerless. I tried to outrun those memories, but they lived inside me.

That is when I learned another kind of escape.

I was not chasing a high — I was chasing absence. I wanted to leave my body altogether. Not die. Just... not be there for a while. Drugs did that. They loosened my grip on reality enough that I could float somewhere else, somewhere nothing hurt.

For someone with no depth perception, the world was already unreliable. Substances made it blurrier, quieter, more forgiving. Or so I thought. But your body does not forget. It does not lie. And it does not forgive easily.

There were moments I should have listened — times my heart raced for no reason, times I felt like I was watching myself from the outside. Dissociation, they call it now. Back then, I just thought I was broken.

I did not understand that trauma does not disappear when you ignore it. It waits. It settles into your bones, your breath, your nervous system. It shows up as anger you cannot explain and sadness that comes out of nowhere. I was carrying years of pain in a body that had never been allowed to rest.

And yet, God was still there.

I did not call Him God then. I did not pray. I did not know how. But there were moments — flashes — when something intervened. A wrong turn that kept me safe. A situation that could have gone so much worse but did not. A sudden urge to leave right before danger arrived.

I chalked it up to luck.

But luck does not follow you that closely. The truth is, I was being protected long before I believed I was worth protecting.

My body started sending louder warnings. Panic attacks before I knew the word for them. Numbness so deep it scared me. I would look in the mirror and not recognize the person staring back. My eyes were there, but I was not. That is when I realized something was wrong — not with the world, but with how I was surviving it.

Still, I did not stop.

Because stopping meant feeling. And feeling meant remembering. And remembering meant facing things I was not ready to name.

So, I kept going, even as my body begged me to slow down. I did not know yet that healing would not come from escaping my body — it would come from learning how to live inside it again. That would take years. And faith. And pain. And grace I had not known yet.

But this was the chapter where my body began to whisper what my soul had been screaming all along: You are not okay. And you do not have to do this alone. I was not listening yet.

There is always a moment when the line gets crossed.

Not a dramatic one. Not the kind you see in movies where alarms go off and everything changes instantly. It is quieter than that. Subtle. A shift so small you do not notice it until you are already on the other side.

For me, it was the first time I realized I could not fully return to who I was before.

I had told myself I was in control. That I could stop whenever I wanted. That I was choosing this life — not being pulled into it. That lie was comfortable. It let me sleep at night. It let me believe I was still steering.

But control does not disappear all at once. It erodes.

Then was the day that started like any other. Same people. Same places. Same ritual. I remember thinking how normal it all felt, which should have scared me more than it did. Normal is dangerous when what you are doing is not.

Something went wrong — not enough to make a good story, but enough to leave a mark. That day, I was given marijuana—tainted with something I still do not know. What I do know is how it felt: the hallucinations, the terror, the sense that I might not survive it. A moment where my body reacted before my mind could. A sudden rush of fear. A sense of slipping away. I remember the ground feeling too far and too close at the same time. Sounds stretched. Time warped.

And then — nothing.

When I came back, all I saw was paramedics all around me. But I knew something had changed. The world felt tilted. Not just visually — spiritually. Like something inside me had shifted out of place. I laughed it off. Made jokes. Put the mask back on. But I knew.

I was not the same.

There was a new awareness now — a knowledge
that I could lose myself completely if I were not
careful. And instead of pulling back, that
realization terrified me into going deeper. Because
once you see how fragile the edge is, standing near
it feels unbearable.

So, I leaned in.

After that, I started noticing how often I
disappeared. Not physically — emotionally.
Conversations I could not remember. Time I could
not account for. A dullness that followed me even
when I was sober. It was like my soul had learned
a new trick: how to leave without permission.

That scared me more than anything.

I would look at my hands and feel disconnected
from them. I would hear my own voice and think it
sounded far away. Mirrors became unsettling —
like the reflection lagged behind the person.

This is what no one tells you about crossing lines:
You do not just risk your life.
You risk your presence.

God was there in that moment too — closer than I
realized. Not condemning. Not angry. Just waiting.
I did not know how to reach for Him yet, but I felt
the space where He should have been. And for the
first time, I missed Him — even though I had not
met Him yet.

That is a strange kind of grief.

I told myself I would be more careful. I told myself I learned my lesson. I told myself a lot of things that were not true.

Because once you cross certain lines, going back is not about willpower anymore. It is about rescue.

I did not know it then, but this was the chapter where I stopped coming back the same — and started inching toward a version of myself I would not recognize.

Not yet.

But soon.

CHAPTER 8 - Camp and The Tall Guy

"Hope deferred makes the heart sick, but a longing fulfilled is a tree of life." — Proverbs 13:12

My mother thought camp would save me.

She thought fresh air, structure, and distance from the streets would straighten out the parts of me that were already bending toward trouble. Maybe she hoped I would come back lighter, happier, easier to love. Or maybe she just needed a break from me and did not know how to say that out loud. So, she signed us up.

Summer camp.

For most kids, camp is memories of bonfires and friendships and inside jokes that last long after August ends. For me, it was the place where my hunger for love finally found a face. That is where I met him. He was tall — impossibly tall to me back then. Six-six, maybe six-seven, with huge feet that seemed to take up half the ground wherever he stood. He walked like he knew where he was going, like the world had already made room for him.

And I noticed him immediately.

Not because he was kind — though sometimes he could be.

Not because he was gentle — he was not.

But because he noticed me.

When you grow up feeling invisible, attention feels like fresh air. He spoke, and I listened.

He decided, and I followed. What he said went — not because I did not have a voice, but because I was desperate to be chosen.

He gave me nicknames — cruel ones. "Princess Dirt" was his favorite.

I laughed when he said it, pretending it did not sting. I wore it like armor, because if I accepted the insult, at least it meant I belonged to him. At least it meant I existed. That is what broken love does. It teaches you to accept pain as proof of connection.

When camp ended, he left for college in Wilkes-Barre, Pennsylvania. He was moving forward. I was stuck. Ninth grade did not survive me — I dropped out. Home felt tighter every day. My mother and I clashed constantly, and I did not know how to explain the ache inside me, so I acted it out instead. Home had become a battlefield. The fighting grew louder. My mother and her boyfriend had no patience left for me — my attitude, my choices, my rebellion. Eventually, they kicked me out. I left with nowhere to land except my father's house. He took me in, but I could not stay long.

While Rick was in college, he told me to come visit. Bus rides. Transfers. Long hours. I traveled miles just to sit at his feet, just to feel close to someone who made me feel wanted — even if it was conditional, even if it hurt.

During that time, I stayed mostly clean. I did not want to lose him. I did not want him to see the parts of me I was already ashamed of. I hid the occasional cocaine use, the pot, the restlessness. I hid the truth the same way I always had — by smiling. Then my body betrayed me.

I missed my period.

Fear crawled up my spine slowly, the way it does when you already know the answer but are not ready to hear it. I was pregnant. Rick's mother was furious. Rick was scared. They sat me down more than once and talked about abortion like it was a simple solution to a complicated problem. Appointment dates were made. Papers were discussed. And every single time I was supposed to go, I got "sick."

Not physically. Spiritually.

Something in me refused to cooperate. I did not know God then. I did not pray. I did not read Scripture. I did not even know how to ask for help. But somehow, something stronger than fear took hold of my heart. I could not do it.

Now I know what that was. It was God stepping in when I could not stand up for myself. He did not abandon me when my home fell apart. He did not leave me when I had nowhere to sleep. He did not turn away when fear dictated my choices. Even when I did not know His name yet, He was making sure I was not alone.

***

"For You created my inmost being;

You knit me together in my mother's womb." —
Psalm 139:13

I did not know that verse then. But I lived it. I
carried everything I owned
in bags that never felt light. My body was changing.
My emotions were wild. My fear grew louder by
the day. I was a child about to have a child, with no
idea how to be one.

Life was unstable everywhere I turned. Rick's
parents took us in next. A roof. A bed. Safety, at
least on the surface. And there, in the middle of
confusion and resentment and fear, my son was
born.

I loved him immediately. Fiercely. Completely.

The moment they placed him in my arms,
something shifted. I did not feel ready. I did not
feel capable. I did not feel strong. But I felt love—
the kind that grabs hold of your soul and refuses to
let go. In that moment, nothing else mattered. Not
the chaos. Not the fear. Not the judgment.

Just him.

I did not know it then, but that love was a glimpse
of God's love for me—a love that stays
even when circumstances fall apart. But you
cannot heal wounds you do not know how to face.
And mine were still wide open. Looking back now,
I can see it clearly: I was not in love with Rick. I
was in love with the idea that someone tall and
strong and certain might fill the holes left by years
of fear, abuse, and neglect. But only God can fill
those places. And He was already moving —
quietly, patiently — even while I kept choosing
people instead of Him.

CHAPTER 9 - A Mother Before I Was Ready

"As a mother comforts her child, so will I comfort you." — Isaiah 66:13

Soon I learned that becoming a mother did not erase my fear. It exposed it.

I loved my son the moment I saw him, but love did not come with instructions. I was young, unsure, and carrying more trauma than I understood. I did not know how to mother because no one had ever shown me how to feel safe myself. Rick and I tried to build something that looked like a family, but cracks showed up fast. We were two broken people pretending responsibility would fix wounds we never addressed. Arguments became routine. Silence became punishment. I felt small again— like the little girl who learned early that love could disappear without warning.

When my daughter came along, the weight doubled. Two children. Two hearts depending on me. And one mother who was still drowning.

I remember holding my babies at night, praying without words, just tears. I wanted to be better. I wanted to be different. I wanted to be the mother they deserved. But wanting is not the same as knowing how.

Rick's temper flared more often. His mother's disappointment was never quiet. I felt judged in every room, measured against expectations I could never reach. Slowly, shame crept in and told me a lie I would believe for years:

You are failing them.

Instead of asking for help, I hid. Instead of admitting fear, I pretended strength. Instead of leaning into God—whom I still barely knew—I leaned into survival.

And survival, for me, had always meant running.

***

The Decision That Still Hurts

I made a decision that still tightens my chest when I think about it. I found another man—someone who promised love, stability, safety. I believed him because I needed to believe someone would save me. I moved out and took my son with me, leaving my daughter with a babysitter. Not because I did not love her. I loved her more than my own breath. But I was overwhelmed. I could not handle two. In my broken thinking, I told myself it was temporary. I told myself I would come back for her once I got steady.

I was wrong.

The man I moved in with was abusive. He hurt me. And later—long after the damage was done—I learned he hurt my son too. That truth shattered

me. Even now, years later, I still pray for healing—
for my son, for myself, for the places that still ache
when I remember. Some wounds take a lifetime to
bring to God, and even then, the scars remain.

"He heals the brokenhearted and binds up their
wounds." — Psalm 147:3

Healing did not happen overnight. It did not come
easily. But God never stopped binding what was
broken—even when I did not know how to ask.

***

The Courtroom Loss

Rick eventually took me to court. We agreed on a
year-on, year-off custody arrangement. I had the
children for the summer. He was supposed to have
them the following year, then they would come
back to me. But that plan never stood a chance. He
moved. He filed in a new court. I never received
the papers. He won by default. Just like that, my
children were gone.

I remember the silence afterward—the kind that
screams. I remember sitting alone, replaying every
decision I ever made, wondering where I went
wrong, wondering if God was punishing me.

Losing my children broke something in me that
drugs had only numbed, never healed. And when
the pain became unbearable, I ran back to the only
thing that ever made the noise stop.

I did not know it then, but even in my worst moments—especially in my worst moments—God was closer than ever. I thought I was falling apart, but He was holding me together. I thought I was beyond saving, but He was writing redemption.

"Can a woman forget her nursing child? ... Even these may forget, yet I will not forget you." — Isaiah 49:15

I felt forgotten. But I was not. And though I could not see it yet, this was not the end of my story.

It was the dark valley before the rescue.

CHAPTER 10 - Back to the Streets

"For I know the plans I have for you, declares the Lord, plans for welfare and not for evil, to give you a future and a hope." Jeremiah 29:11

Drugs did not knock on the door. They were waiting for me. I did not use because I wanted to party. I used because I wanted the pain to stop screaming. I wanted sleep without dreams. I wanted a few hours where my heart did not feel like it was being torn open.

Kensington welcomed me back without questions.

The streets do not judge you for being broken— they expect it. I blended in easily. Too easily. I knew how to survive there. I knew which corners were safe, who to avoid, how to disappear when police lights flashed. I hid pipes in my underwear. If I accidentally dropped drugs on the ground, I would scrape at the dirt, desperate to recover whatever piece of relief I had lost.

More than once, I was stopped by police—my heart racing, my body shaking—only to be waved on. Grace! I did not deserve, and mercy I did not recognize at the time.

"Surely goodness and mercy shall follow me all the days of my life." — Psalm 23:6

Even there, mercy followed me.

I became invisible on purpose. I did not want to be seen. I did not want to be known. I did not want anyone to look close enough to see the mother who lost her children or the woman who could not stop destroying herself. I watched people walk by—clean clothes, steady jobs, full lives—and wondered why they did not care about me. Or maybe they did and chose not to do anything.

I would have given anything for a hug.
A handshake.
A moment of human kindness.

But I did not ask. I learned a long time ago not to expect much.

***

God Was Still Whispering

I did not feel God in those days. I did not hear Him. I did not pray. I did not believe He wanted anything to do with me. But looking back now, I know this truth:

The enemy was shouting, but God was whispering.

Whispering through the fact that I was still alive. Whispering through every overdose I survived. Whispering through every night I should not have made it home. Whispering through strangers who helped me when they did not have to. I thought I had fallen too far, but God never lost sight of me.

"Where can I go from Your Spirit?
Where can I flee from Your presence?" — Psalm
139:7

I ran hard.
I ran far.

And He stayed.

***

The Bottom Has a Basement

The streets did not heal me. They consumed me.
Drugs stopped working the way they use to. What
once numbed pain began to multiply it. My body
broke down. My mind grew darker. Hope felt like
something meant for other people. And that is
when God did something I never expected.

He let me hit the bottom.

Not because He was cruel, but because He was
preparing a way out. I did not know it yet, but a
miracle was coming. Not loud. Not flashy.

Just a phonebook...
and a moment that would start something new.

CHAPTER 11 - The Phonebook and The Door God Opened

"He lifted me out of the slimy pit, out of the mud
and mire; He set my feet on a rock
and gave me a firm place to stand." — Psalm 40:2

Rock bottom does not always look dramatic. Sometimes it looks like sitting alone in a room that smells like defeat, your body exhausted, your soul hollowed out, knowing you cannot keep living the way you are—but having no idea how to stop.

That is where I was.

I was not looking for God. I was just tired. Tired of running. Tired of numbing. Tired of surviving instead of living. I remember grabbing a phonebook—one of those thick, outdated ones people barely use anymore. I did not have a plan. I did not even know what I was searching for. I just opened it.

And there it was.

Rehab. Right in front of me. Clear. Obvious. As if it had been waiting for me the whole time. I stared at the page for a long moment, my heart pounding. I wish I could tell you I felt hope. I did not. What I felt was fear. Fear of change. Fear of failure. Fear of sobriety. Fear of facing myself without anything to hide behind. But something in me dialed the number anyway.That was not courage. That was desperation. And desperation, I have learned, is often the doorway God uses when pride will not budge.

***

I lasted about two weeks. Two weeks of meetings. Two weeks of structure. Two weeks of hearing my own story in other people's voices. Two weeks of being forced to sit still with pain I had buried for decades. I convinced myself I was healed. I convinced myself I was different. I convinced myself I did not need to be there anymore. That is what pride sounds like when it borrows confidence.

So, I left.

And as soon as I stepped back into the world, reality reminded me of a truth I did not want to accept I was not healed. I was just sober long enough to lie to myself. Looking back now, I can see how gently God handled me. He did not punish me for leaving rehab early. He did not abandon me because I was not ready.

He waited.

He watched me try again—and fail again. He watched me circle the same pain, the same patterns, the same lies. And He stayed.

"The Lord is compassionate and gracious, slow to anger, abounding in love." — Psalm 103:8

I did not understand grace yet. I thought God worked on a strike system—three failures and you are out. But God does not keep score the way humans do.

Not long after leaving rehab, I found myself in another relationship. Another marriage. Another promise that this time things would be different. He was an addict too. Cocaine. Crack. I stayed clean for a little while—long enough to feel the familiar itch return. Long enough to hear the lie whisper: If you cannot beat him, join him.

And so, I did.

Back on drugs I went. Not because I did not know better. But because pain was louder than wisdom. Even then, God was not done with me. He was not shocked by my relapse. He was not surprised by my weakness. He was not finished writing my story. I thought I was running away from Him. But the truth is...He was walking with me through it all, waiting for the moment my heart would finally look up instead of down.

"If we are faithless, He remains faithful, for He cannot deny Himself." — 2 Timothy 2:13

I was not ready yet, but I was getting closer. And God knew exactly how much it would take to bring me home.

CHAPTER 12 - Running Again, This Time to Virginia

"I have surely seen the affliction of My people... and I have come down to deliver them." — Exodus 3:7–8

When that marriage finally collapsed, I felt the familiar urge to run. Running had always been my answer—new places, new people, new beginnings that I hoped would erase old mistakes. This time, my heart pulled me south.

Virginia.

Maybe I could rescue something there. Maybe I could fix my relationship with my mother, a relationship that had been broken and patched so many times it barely held together anymore. Maybe distance from the streets, from the memories, from the people who knew my worst moments would save me. So, I packed up what little I had left and went.

At first, things looked almost... normal. I was clean again. I had a place to stay. I felt cautious hope, the kind you do not speak out-loud because you are afraid you will jinx it. My sister needed a place to live, and I wanted to help. I thought maybe this was a chance to heal something old, something deep. So, I brought her to Virginia with me.

For a while, it worked. We shared a townhouse. I tried to build a routine. I tried to be stable. I tried to believe that maybe—just maybe—this time I had finally outrun my past. But broken people do not always heal well together.

One day, I came home to silence. The townhouse was empty. My sister was gone. And so was everything else. Not just her things. Mine too: furniture, belongings, pieces of my life I had slowly rebuilt. What she left behind was mess and wreckage—emotional and physical. I stood there staring at the empty rooms, feeling like the wind had been knocked out of me. Later, I would learn she had gone to my mother and told untruths— stories twisted by old wounds and unresolved pain. Whatever fragile healing my mother and I had managed to build shattered again. I realized then something painful but important: some people are not meant to walk every part of your healing journey with you.

Cleaning that townhouse became more than just picking up broken pieces—it was symbolic. I was cleaning up my life again. Starting again. Alone again. But this time, something was different. I did not immediately run back to drugs. I did not immediately self-destruct. I sat in the quiet and felt the pain instead.

"Be still and know that I am God." — Psalm 46:10

Stillness had always terrified me. Stillness meant feeling. Stillness meant memories. Stillness meant hearing my own thoughts. But God was teaching me something new. He was teaching me how to stand—not on people, not on places, not on substances—but on Him.

I did not know it yet, but I was standing on the edge of a season that would finally change everything. Because when the running finally slowed, God was ready to show me who I was meant to be.

CHAPTER 13 - Positive Paws: Building Something That Did Not Hurt Me

"Commit to the Lord whatever you do, and He will establish your plans." — Proverbs 16:3

By the time I created Positive Paws K9 Training, I had already lost more than most people ever will. I was not young anymore. I was not chasing dreams fueled by naivety. I was building something out of necessity—out of survival—out of the quiet hope that maybe I could create a life that did not constantly fall apart. Dog training had followed me for years, in and out of seasons of my life. But this time was different. This time, I did not just want a job. I wanted something mine. Something that did not hurt me. Something that did not leave. Something that did not betray me. I wanted a place where trust mattered. That is how Positive Paws K9 Training was born. I did not start with money, investors, or even confidence; I started with experience, instinct, and a deep understanding of fear—both canine and human.

I trained dogs wherever I could. I hustled. I cleaned. I showed up early and stayed late. I built relationships one dog at a time, one family at a time. Word spread quickly, not because I was flashy, but because I was effective. People saw something in the way I worked with dogs. I did not overpower them; I did not scare them, and I certainly did not rush them. I met them where they were. Because no one had ever done that for me—and I knew how much it mattered.

Positive Paws was more than a name; it was not just branding—it was a philosophy. It was the opposite of how I had been treated most of my life. No fear-based control. No punishment-first thinking. No dominance masquerading as leadership. I believed—deeply—that healing came through consistency, boundaries, patience, and love. Dogs proved me right every day: reactive dogs softened, fearful dogs gained confidence, and aggressive dogs learned calm. And as they healed, something unexpected happened: so did I. Every success reminded me that broken things can be rebuilt. That behavior is not identity. That fear does not get the final word.

"The Lord will perfect that which concerns me." — Psalm 138:8

At some point, I looked around and realized—I was not just training dogs anymore. I was running a business. Clients depended on me. Employees looked to me. Dogs trusted me. Schedules, payments, responsibility—it was all mine. And for the first time in my life, I did not run from it; I rose to it. I was making good money. Honest money. I was respected for something that came naturally to me. I woke up with purpose instead of dread. I went to bed tired in a good way—the kind of tired that comes from doing something meaningful. Positive Paws became a place of safety—not just for dogs, but for me.

I do not remember the exact moment it happened, but I remember the feeling: Pride. Not the loud kind. Not arrogance. The quiet kind that whispers "you did this. You stayed. You did not quit." I had built something with my hands, my heart, and my hard-earned wisdom. I had taken years of pain and turned it into skill. Years of fear and turned it into empathy. And even though I did not fully understand it yet, God was smiling. He was using something I loved to prepare me for something bigger.

God was expanding the vision! Positive Paws did not stop at obedience training. We expanded into daycare, behavioral rehabilitation, and eventually service dog training. My heart leaned toward the dogs that needed the most patience—the ones everyone else had given up on, because I knew what it felt like to be written off. Looking back now, I see it clearly: Positive Paws was not just a business. It was a bridge. A bridge from survival to purpose. From chaos to consistency. From brokenness to calling.

And it was there—inside the walls of something I built—that God sent a scared white German Shepherd puppy named Branco...

...and the doctor who would become my sister.

"Being confident of this, that He who began a good work in you will carry it on to completion." — Philippians 1:6

Positive Paws was never just about dogs; it was about God showing me that I could build something that lasted, and that He was not finished building me.

CHAPTER 14 - The Man I Never Wanted (But GOD Clearly Did)

"The Lord directs our steps, so why try to understand everything along the way?" — Proverbs 20:24 (paraphrased)
(Because if I had understood this one, I would've run.)

Before I continue with my Branco story, let me mention something that had happened just before this puppy showed up. But let me start by making something very clear: I was not looking for another man; I was not praying for him, and I was not expecting him! And if God had asked my opinion first, I would have said, "Absolutely not. Please and thank you."

He was a little older than me. And by *a little*, I mean enough that my grandkids feel comfortable roasting him without remorse. He rides a Harley. He is rough around the edges. And his dog's name was Harley — because of course it was. That should have been my sign.

I met him through dog training. Training his puppy was fun. Training him was not. He asked me out for pizza, and I said yes. I meant no. So, I did not show up. Then he asked again. And again, I did not show up. Then again. At this point, I thought he would take the hint. But no. This man had the audacity to be patient. Calm. Persistent. Sir... what is wrong with you?

Now let us address the elephant on his head. He is a little bit bald. Not according to him — according to my grandkids. They say he does not have hair; he has whiskers on his head. I try to defend him and say he is just thinning. He says he is "seasoned."

He attempts a comb-over like no one notices. Like gravity has not already spoken. I have seen that comb-over fight the wind — and lose. Every. Single. Time.

The kids are brutal.

"Papa, why does your hair start back there?"
"Papa, is your head cold?"
"Papa, did you forget to finish your haircut?"

And Eddie just sighs and says,
"Y'all lucky I love your grandma."

Which is fair.

***

The moment I realized he was not leaving was not cute; I had all my upper teeth pulled. All of them. I do not know if I have said this before, but after the fall down the steps—when I was three years old—I began having seizures. One ordinary day, a seizure took me down again. Only this time, I fell forward. The damage was severe—my teeth fractured, the break reaching all the way into my jawbone. I was swollen, bloody, miserable, drooling, crying, looking like a medical emergency with feelings. I resembled a crime scene more than a woman.

And guess who stayed?

Him.

He stayed the night while I cried, complained, bled, and questioned every life decision I had ever made. He did not gag. He did not panic. He did not flee. He stayed. No man had ever stayed with me at my worst. Men stayed when I was fun; they stayed when I was wild or when I was broken in ways they could control. But this? This was not cute, and he stayed anyway, which terrified me. This felt suspicious…Here is the problem: I was used to chaos, drama, and pain disguised as passion. If love did not hurt a little, I did not trust it, and Eddie did not hurt. He did not yell. He did not disappear. He did not control. He was steady. And honestly? That made me nervous. I kept waiting for the other shoe to drop. I kept checking for red flags. I kept thinking, *Sir, where is the trauma? Where is the chaos?*

But he was just… there. Consistent. Loyal. Unbothered.

"Love is patient, love is kind… it always perseveres." — 1 Corinthians 13:4,7

Turns out patience feels weird when you have lived in survival mode your whole life. Looking back now, I know this truth: God was laughing. Because the man I never wanted was the man I needed, not to save me or to fix me, but to show me that love does not have to hurt to be real. He might be losing his hair, but he never lost his character.

And God knew exactly what He was doing — because He sent me a man secure enough to laugh at himself, strong enough to stay, and stubborn enough to love me even when I tried to dodge him. I asked God for peace; and He sent me a Harley-riding, comb-over-defending, whisker-headed man who stayed when things got ugly. And honestly? That is divine comedy at its finest.

CHAPTER 15 - She Came in Like a Hurricane (and Her Sidekick Was Branco)

"God sets the lonely in families." — Psalm 68:6 (Sometimes He delivers them on a leash.)

The day Katy came into my life, she did not gently enter. She blew in.

The door opened and in walked this very quiet woman holding onto a leash attached to what can only be described as a four-legged natural disaster: Fifteen weeks old, White German Shepherd, all paws, no coordination, and zero confidence. His name was Branco. He immediately slipped on the floor, panicked, tried to flee, realized the leash existed, and then froze like the world had betrayed him personally. And I fell in love on the spot.

Katy stood there calmly, politely, apologetically, while her puppy unraveled in real time. She had this look on her face that said, I am a doctor... I have made a terrible mistake. She introduced herself softly. Her accent gave her away — El Salvador — but her English was better than mine. She was reserved, composed, kind, and wildly unprepared.

***

For a German Shepherd, Branco was the least intimidating creature alive.

A loud noise? Trauma.
A new surface? Absolutely not.
A leaf moving in the breeze? Immediate suspicion.

This dog was convinced the world was out to get
him. Big body; tiny courage. Katy watched him like
she was waiting for instructions from the universe.
I watched her and thought, Oh honey... you have
no idea what you just signed up for.

Here is the thing about Katy. She is very book
smart: medical school, degrees, intelligence that
could diagnose you from across the room. Street
smarts? None. Zero. Nada.

Blessed.
Highly favored.
Absolutely lacking common sense.

She stood there politely while her puppy tried to
self-destruct, asking thoughtful questions, listening
carefully, trusting me instantly. A doctor... trusting
me? God has jokes.

Within five minutes, it was obvious: Katy is quiet; I
am not. Katy thinks things through; I feel things
out. Katy trusts people; I trust patterns. She
believes the best in everyone; I believe people
show you exactly who they are — usually quickly.
She would stop to help a stranger waving her
down in a dark parking lot; I would already be in
the car yelling, "WHY ARE WE STOPPING?" She
thinks I am dramatic. I think she is going to get us

both kidnapped. We balance each other beautifully.

***

Branco: The Icebreaker God Used

Week after week, Katy came back. Branco got bigger. Still scared. Still goofy. Still dramatic. And every week, Katy watched me work with him — how I slowed down, how I did not rush, how I did not force him to be brave before he was ready. She trusted me, and that mattered more than she probably realized because trust had not been a common gift in my life.

And somewhere between training sessions, conversations, and watching her realize she was in over her head with a very large baby dinosaur, something shifted. She asked me to go hiking with her and a friend. I froze. A doctor… asking me to hang out? Why? People like her did not usually choose people like me. But I said yes. And that yes would change everything.

I thought I was training a puppy.

God was introducing me to:
- A sister
- A prayer warrior
- A built-in conscience
- A family I did not know I needed

And He used a scared white German Shepherd named Branco to do it.

"A man's heart plans his way, but the Lord directs his steps." — Proverbs 16:9

My steps were being redirected. And the hurricane that walked in with a leash? She had only just made landfall.

CHAPTER 16 – Hikes, Friendship, and the Snail

"As iron sharpens iron, so one person sharpens another." Proverbs 27:17

The hikes did not start as anything meaningful. They were not spiritual or intentional; they were not even my idea. They were just walks. Katy would text something casual like, "Branco needs to burn energy. Want to hike?" And I would say yes — not because I loved hiking, but because saying yes felt easier than sitting alone with my thoughts. Branco was still growing into himself then. Too big for his confidence. All legs, no coordination. Easily startled, deeply dramatic. He approached the woods like they might personally offend him. Every snapping twig was suspicious. Every rustle meant danger. Every incline required emotional preparation. Watching him figure out the world felt... familiar. He wanted to be brave; he just did not know how yet.

Katy does not fill silence; she is comfortable in it. At first, that made me uneasy. I was used to noise — filling space, controlling the room, staying ahead of my own thoughts. Silence had never been safe for me. But on the trail, silence felt different: the crunch of gravel, leaves shifting in the wind, Branco stopping every five feet to reassess his life choices. No pressure. No fixing. No explaining. Just movement.

We walked a lot. Different trails, different seasons, but the same rhythm. And somewhere between the uphill breathing and the downhill quiet, something inside me started to soften. At the time, I would not have called it God, but I felt something steady, a calm I did not have to earn, a presence that did not demand anything from me.

Branco started to change, too. The dog who once froze at shadows started walking ahead. The puppy who flinched at noise began to lead; fear softened into curiosity. That showed me change does not have to be accompanied by pain. Step by step, trail by trail, God was preparing my heart — not through sermons, but through presence, through a quiet doctor, a scared white German Shepherd, and a path that asked nothing from me except to keep walking.

***

Hiking with Katy had become a regular thing. Fresh air. Trails. Nature. Branco learning that the world exists outside his comfort zone. It was healthy. Grounding. Spiritual, even. Which should have been my first clue something was about to go wrong. We came to a river crossing — nothing dramatic. Not wide. Not deep. Just one of those moments where the trail says, Figure it out. The water moved steadily, rocks visible beneath the surface. Easy enough.

Katy went first. She stepped across confidently, like a person who trusts nature and has never been personally betrayed by it. Branco followed, suspicious but obedient. Then it was my turn.

I stepped into the water. I was halfway across when Katy suddenly yelled:

"GO. GO. GO. GO. GO."

Not screamed. Not panicked. Urgent. Commanding. Like someone who had just seen something she did not want to explain. I froze for half a second — because that is my brand — then crossed faster than dignity allows, water splashing, arms flailing slightly, pride completely abandoned. I made it to the other side breathing hard.

"WHAT?" I asked.

Katy smiled. A calm smile. The kind that should concern you. And then — very casually — Katy said:

"Oh. There was a snake."

I stared at her.

"A snake?" I repeated.

"Yes," she said. "Under the rock. Right where you stepped."

I blinked. Slowly. "You mean... was there a snake?" I asked.

"No," she said. "There is a snake."

I looked back at the river. The rock. The water. The exact place my foot had been. I felt the delayed adrenaline hit — the kind that arrives late but loud.

"You could've told me BEFORE," I said.

She shrugged. "I needed you to move."

Here's the thing. If she had told me, "There is a snake under that rock," I would have:

- screamed
- fallen
- drowned
- died dramatically

Instead, I crossed safely. Because I did not know. Ignorance, in this case, was protection. I realized something important right then. Katy does not panic. She assesses; she acts and then explains later. I panic, overthink, ask too many questions; I would like advance notice for danger, please and thank you.

Together? We survive. She sees the threat. I move when told. And nobody dies. Not all protection comes with explanations. Likewise, sometimes God does not tell you why — He just says,

"Move."

And you do not find out what you avoided until you are already safe. We do not need to see the snake. We do not need to understand the danger. We just need to cross.

***

And then there was the snail... I was almost killed by a snail.

That sentence alone tells you two important things about my life:

1. Chaos has excellent timing.
2. I survive things I have no business surviving.

It happened on a Sunday that was supposed to be calm. A tubing trip. Sunshine. A river. Lunch packed in a cooler like we were responsible adults. My husband, my best friend, and me—floating along, pretending we were people whose lives moved in straight lines.

We were drifting peacefully, talking about nothing important, when I had a thought — the kind of thought that only visits me during moments of calm.

I should be funny.

I do not know why I do this. When life finally relaxes, I poke it. Like a cat knocking a glass off a table just to watch gravity work. So, when everything was going well, I did what I tend to do in moments like that—I introduced unnecessary chaos. I put a small hole in my husband's tube. A joke. A tiny one. Barely a crime. The tube deflated immediately. Aggressively. Like it had been waiting for this moment.

The plan was simple. Watch it slowly deflate. Laugh. Say something like, "That's weird, what's happening to your tube?" and pretend innocence.

My husband was not amused. Not even a little.

So, being generous, I gave him my tube, and Katy and I decided to share one because clearly we were thinking clearly. That plan lasted approximately three seconds.

The tube flipped. On the rapids.

Suddenly, Katy and I were underwater, tangled, disoriented, and immediately reevaluating our entire friendship. I instinctively covered my head with my arms — thank God — and launched out of the water like a human torpedo.

"I THINK I BROKE MY ARM!" I yelled.

Blood poured down my arm like I had auditioned for a low-budget horror movie. Then my body decided to add a bonus feature. A seizure. Then another. Back-to-back. Katy holding on to me for dear life. Chaos erupted. A stranger — an actual angel in swim trunks — jumped off his tube without hesitation and grabbed me. My husband, safely floating nearby, yelled, "IS SHE OKAY?" while remaining exactly where he was. Because he cannot swim. Katy was still holding me above water, terrified, focused, and likely reconsidering every life decision that led her to this moment. Eventually, my husband and the stranger, who happened to be a firefighter, saved me.

Once in the Emergency Room, the doctor ordered X-rays. The nurse takes me to get them and brings me back to the room. When she came back, she looked confused and amused at the same time. Which is never what you want.

"This is a first," she said. "You didn't break your arm," she continued.

Okay… good?

Then she took us in to see the X-ray and pointed to the massive swelling.

"That," she said, "is a snail."

A snail. Not on my arm. In my arm.

Somehow, when my arm hit the riverbed, a snail lodged itself into my flesh. And yes — they had to cut it out. And yes — Katy still has the snail. Because of course she does.

So let us recap:

• I sabotaged my husband's tube

• I almost drowned

• I seized in a river, twice

• A stranger saved my life

• My husband supervised loudly from a safe distance

• And I was taken out by a snail

On a relaxing Sunday.

Later, I laughed — not because it was funny at the time, but because laughing meant I survived. Chaos did not win this round. My life has never moved in straight lines. It flips tubes. Introduces unnecessary snails. And somehow leaves me with another story I did not ask for but cannot forget.

If nothing else, this is what I know:

God has a sense of humor. Because of all the ways to remind me I am human, fragile, and very much not in control... He chose a snail.

CHAPTER 17 - Excuses, Excuses (And God Still Showed Up)

"Here I am! I stand at the door and knock." —
Revelation 3:20
(I heard the knock. I just pretended I was not
home.)

Katy never stopped asking.

"Do you want to study the Bible with me?"
"Do you want to come to church?"
"Do you want to listen to this sermon?"

And I never stopped answering. Just not with yes.

I went here and there—every once in a while—
enough to say I tried. Enough to quiet her concern.
Enough to convince myself I was open, even
though I was not.

I always had an excuse: I was tired, I was busy, I
had work, I had dogs, I had life. And if I am being
honest? I did not think God had been with me
anyway.

I had a whole system.

If she asked on a Sunday:
"I'm exhausted."

If she asked midweek:
"I'm slammed with work."

If she asked again:
"I'll go next time."

There was always a next time. Just never a now. I told myself I did not have time for God. But the truth was harder to admit... I did not think God had time for me. I looked at my life—abuse, addiction, losing my kids, the streets, the relapses—and thought, If God was with me, surely it would not have looked like this. So, I stayed busy. Busy is a great hiding place.

But Katy was not buying it. Katy, being Katy, did not argue. She did not guilt me. She did not preach at me. She did not push. She just kept inviting, calm, consistent, annoyingly patient. She would say things like "I'll be praying for you." Which somehow felt worse than pressure because prayer meant she believed God was still listening for me—even when I was not listening for Him.

Here is the lie I carried for years: God shows up for good people, and I did not think I qualified. I thought faith was for people with clean stories, neat timelines, and testimonies that did not come with footnotes and court records. I thought God might tolerate me... but walk with me? That felt like a stretch so, I kept Him at arm's length. Close enough to acknowledge; far enough to avoid disappointment.

What I did not realize then was this: God had been with me the whole time.

In the streets.
In the overdoses I survived.
In the moments I should have died.
In the dogs I trained.
In the people He placed beside me, especially Katy.

"The Lord is compassionate and gracious, slow to anger, abounding in love." — Psalm 103:8

I was not rejecting God; I was afraid to trust Him, because trusting Him meant admitting that maybe—just maybe—He never left. And that meant everything I thought I knew about my life... was about to change.

***

The Day I Could not Run from Katy

I invited Katy to go away for the weekend with me and a young boy named Mason, who always helped me out whenever he was home from school. I thought it would be a simple escape—a break from life. We headed to my campground, planning to relax and try our hand at crabbing, even though none of us actually knew how to crab. Mason was excited. He had his heart set on it. Katy, on the other hand, had different plans.

Instead of giving me space, she held me hostage— in the best way possible—and drilled straight into my head, filling it with the Good News. This time, it stuck. I could not run. There was nowhere to hide.

She explained Scripture, piece by piece, truth by truth. At night, I went to bed exhausted but unable to sleep, replaying everything she had said, turning it over in my mind.

The next morning, I made breakfast. We dropped more crab pots into the river and headed back to the RV. Before I realized it, we were deep in the Word. I was not just listening anymore—I was asking questions, commenting, engaging. Somewhere between the coffee and the conversation, something shifted. I guess a weekend without an escape was exactly what I needed. And that is when I gave my life to Jesus.

Then, a crime scene waiting for us... well kind of...

We walked back down to the river, pulled up the cages, and there they were—CRABS. Actual crabs. Alive. Moving. Staring at us like, Well? Now what?

We had no idea how to cook them. None. But Mason wanted to try, so there we were—well, Katy really—boiling water and dropping crabs in one by one. We were yelling. Crying. Laughing. Traumatized. It felt like we were committing murder in slow motion. It was chaos. I wish I could show you the video, because it was honestly one of the funniest moments of my life. A weekend that started with me trying to get away ended with

Scripture, surrender, and a very dramatic crab boil.

And somehow, God was in all of it.

We came back home. Katy and I studied Scripture together. We listened to teachings. I asked questions I had avoided for years. I was not trying to become perfect; I was trying to be free. I wanted to leave my past behind me. For the first time, I was not running. A few weeks later, I asked Katy if her father, a preacher, would baptize me. He stood beside me at the lake. I went under the water; I let go. When I came back up, I felt clean in a way I never had before.

CHAPTER 18 - The Place I Built was Taken from Me

"Even my close friend, someone I trusted, one who shared my bread, has turned against me." — Psalm 41:9

Positive Paws did not fall apart all at once. It cracked first; hairline fractures I ignored because I was tired. Because I trusted people when I should not have. Because I believed doing good meant people would do right by me. I was wrong. I had built Positive Paws with my own hands—through long days, sleepless nights, and years of experience earned the hard way. It was not just a business. It was proof that I could create something that did not hurt me. That I could stay. That I could succeed. And then I invited people in. That was my mistake.

***

The Nonprofit Dream

We decided to expand—service dogs, mission-driven work, helping others the way dogs had helped me. It felt right. It felt like purpose. We formed a nonprofit, moved to a bigger building that Katy got, invited people to join, trusted that shared vision meant shared integrity. It did not. I did not see the shift at first. Conversations changed, meetings felt off, decisions were questioned—not in healthy ways, but in controlling ones. I started to feel like a guest in the place I built. Still, I stayed quiet. I had spent a lifetime being told I was "too much," so when something felt wrong, I swallowed it. I told myself I was being paranoid. Dramatic. Broken-brained from past trauma. That lie cost me everything.

Then COVID hit. Clients disappeared overnight, daycare emptied, training schedules collapsed. I did what every small business owner was told to do to survive—I applied for PPP loans. They were approved. Later, I was told I could receive a second loan. No paperwork needed, they said. I trusted that advice. I trusted the process. I trusted the people around me. That trust would be used against me. When business did not bounce back the way we hoped, blame started to circulate, quiet conversations, side glances, whispers I was not meant to hear—but did. And then one of the very people I had brought in—someone sitting on the board—turned me in. Fraud, they said. Just like that.

***

I had never been arrested in my life. Never. And suddenly, I was standing in a courtroom, indicted. My name dragged through something that felt unreal. Like I was watching someone else's nightmare. The first charge was dropped—we had proof. Documentation. Truth.

But the second one? There was no paper trail. So, I took a plea. Not because I was guilty of what they accused me of—but because I was exhausted. Broken. Out of money. Out of fight. I was arrested. Me. The woman who had spent her life trying to outrun shame now had to stand inside it.

I lost everything. My money, my reputation, my business. I spent a year on house arrest, confined to the walls of what used to feel like safety. I was done. I did not want to fight anymore. I did not want to wake up anymore.

***

"A friend is always loyal, and a brother (or a sister) is born to help in time of need" Proverbs 17:17.

"Where Is the Gun?"

I remember the thoughts clearly. Where is the gun? Where are the drugs? Just leave me alone. I was not dramatic. I was empty. I tried to isolate. That has always been my instinct—disappear quietly so no one has to watch me fall apart. But Katy would not let me. She did not lecture. She did not fix. She did not rush me. She sat with me and cried with me. She reminded me—over and over—that what happened to me was not who I was. But I did not want to believe that. And when I told her I was done—done trying, done believing, done living the way I had been—she heard what I was not saying. She knew I was in danger, so she stepped in and brought me to her house. And for a while, that is where I stayed—held together by prayer when I was not strong enough to pray myself.

"Bear one another's burdens, and so fulfill the law of Christ." — Galatians 6:2

She carried mine when I could not. We cried—not polite tears, not quiet ones. The kind of crying that comes from losing everything you believed God gave you. I told Him I was done. And for the first time, I meant it. What I could not see in that moment—but can see now—is that God did not betray me. People did. And He allowed the collapse not because He was cruel—but because He was not going to let my identity stay tied to something that could be taken away.

"The Lord is close to the brokenhearted and saves those who are crushed in spirit." — Psalm 34:18

Positive Paws collapsed, but I did not. Not completely. Because even in the betrayal, even in the silence, even in the humiliation— God was still holding me. And the story was not over.

CHAPTER 19 - Again, I Had Nothing

"Naked I came from my mother's womb, and naked I will depart.
The Lord gave and the Lord has taken away; may the name of the Lord be praised." — Job 1:21

Again... everything was gone.

I had nothing. No business, no money, no reputation, no future I could see. Just silence. I had lived this before—many times, actually—but this loss hit differently. This time, it was not drugs that took everything. It was not chaos or recklessness. It was not even my past. This time, it was betrayal, and that cut deeper. I sat in rooms that still echoed with dreams I had spoken out loud. Plans I had prayed over. Work I had poured myself into. I replayed every decision, every conversation, every moment I ignored my gut because I wanted to believe people were good.

I felt stupid.
Naive.
Ashamed.

Not because I had failed—but because I had trusted.

***

Starting over once is brave. Starting over twice is exhausting. Starting over again feels cruel. I did not have the energy to rebuild. I did not have the strength to dream. I did not even have the anger left to fight. I just felt... empty.

There were moments I stared at the ceiling and wondered how much more God expected me to survive. I did not ask out loud. I did not cry dramatically. I just wondered quietly. Why does everything I build get taken away from me? Why does hope keep costing me so much?
Shame is sneaky. It whispered things like: You should have known better, this always happens to you, or you are the common denominator. I started believing that maybe God only let me borrow good things for a while—never long enough to keep them. I thought maybe this was my punishment for all the years I ran from Him, maybe this was what I deserved. But even in that darkness, something small stayed alive inside me. A flicker. Just breath. And sometimes, that is enough.

When everything is gone, something strange happens. You stop pretending, you stop performing strength, you stop explaining yourself, you stop trying to impress God. You just sit there and tell Him the truth. And the truth was simple:

"I can't do this anymore."

I did not hear an answer or felt relief, but I did not die either. And that mattered. Because even when I had nothing— no identity, no plans, no ground beneath me— I still had breath. And breath means God is not finished.

***

Katy had just left a medical practice. She was standing on the edge of something new—about to step out on her own and start her own medical practice. That alone was terrifying and exciting all at once. And there I was—health failing, strength fading, barely holding myself together. So, during the day I stayed at the building with her. Not because it was convenient but because she needed to keep an eye on her sister: Me. We did not say it aloud, but we both knew I was not okay. My body was struggling. My spirit was worse, being alone was not safe. Katy never made me feel like a burden. She never treated me like a patient. She just made space. And somehow, in that space, God began to work.

CHAPTER 20 - When I Spoke His Name

"Submit yourselves therefore to God. Resist the devil, and he will flee from you." — James 4:7

Walking away from what I was born into was not loud. It did not involve shouting or chasing darkness; it involved truth. And truth has a name: Jesus.

I thought I had given my life completely to God before everything fell apart. I had prayed with Katy's dad, and he baptized me. But it was not until God stripped everything else away—until He was all I had—that I truly surrendered completely.

Jesus is enough. I no longer need to chase anything. I do not need guidance from the stars, messages from spirits, fake relationships, or numbing from drugs. All I needed is Jesus, and He does not demand anything from me except my heart. And God worked patiently, layer by layer, healing my heart from the wounds I carried.

"If you confess with your mouth that Jesus is Lord and believe in your heart that God raised Him from the dead, you will be saved." — Romans 10:9

CHAPTER 21 - When Pastor Debbie Called

"The Lord is near to the brokenhearted and saves the crushed in spirit." — Psalm 34:18

The building that once housed Positive Paws now stood empty. Katy put the building on the market. Legally, it was hers. The special use permit, however, was in my name. And since they had served me with a no trespassing order, preventing me from continuing my dog training business in the very building we had worked so hard for, they were no longer allowed to remain there either. The building remained in the market for several months, nothing happened. I hated that building— not because of Katy, but because of what it represented: loss, humiliation, another ending I did not ask for. Katy believed—steadily, quietly— that God had slammed the door on us for something bigger. Something we could not see yet. I did not know it then, but she had been praying for a church to buy that building.

***

That afternoon felt like many others had lately. Katy and I were sitting together in her office— probably listening to Christian music, like we had been doing more and more those days. Worship had become our background noise. Prayer had become our reflex. We talked quietly. Sometimes we did not talk at all.

There was no grand plan, no five-year vision—just trust built one day at a time. We had prayed over that building so many times. Not for profit. Not for restoration. Just that God would put the right people there. People who would honor Him, and then the phone rang.

◻

"Hello?" - I answered without expectation.

A woman's voice came through the line—warm, calm, steady.

"Hi... are you the owner of the building on Churchman's Mill Road?"

Something in me paused.

"Yes," I said. She continued, "My name is Debbie. I pastor Emerge Ministries, and we have been praying about space. We were wondering if you would consider renting the building to us."

A church! Calling us. In that building.

I looked at Katy. She looked at me. Neither of us spoke, but we both knew—this was not coincidence. This was God! There are moments when faith requires trust. And then there are moments when God makes Himself undeniable.

***

When Pastor Debbie came to see the building, she did not walk through it like someone negotiating square footage. She walked through it like someone sensing holy ground. She did not start with numbers; she did not rush logistics. She talked about people. About souls. About calling. And something settled in my spirit. God was not giving me back what I lost. He was redeeming where I had bled.

"The stone the builders rejected has become the cornerstone." — Psalm 118:22

When Emerge Ministries moved in, the atmosphere changed. The building that once echoed with loss now echoed with worship. The space that held my breaking now held God's work. And I finally understood something I had not before: God did not abandon me when everything collapsed. He cleared the room.

CHAPTER 22 - I Walked Back In

"Surely the Lord was in this place, and I did not know it." — Genesis 28:16

It was hard for me to go into that building for a good while. Even after Pastor Debbie called and after the prayers were answered, even after the doors opened again with new purpose. That building held too much memory. Too much loss. Too much of who I used to be when everything fell apart. Walking past it stirred grief I was not sure I was ready to face. But one day, Katy and I went to Emerge Ministries Sunday service. And let me tell you—it was incredible.

The worship filled the space in a way it never had before. The walls that once witnessed my pain now resounded with praise. Where there had been silence and sorrow, there was joy, laughter, and hope. I stood there quietly, taking it all in, my heart pounding, my eyes filling with tears. It felt like God had taken everything that had broken me in that building and breathed life back into it. It took me a minute, and a whole lot of prayer. But eventually, something settled deep in my spirit. Emerge Ministries was not just in that building. It was now my church.

***

Now let us talk about Pastor Debbie. She is short, but do not let that fool you. That woman is powerful. Like... I genuinely believe she has TNT in her blood, because when the Holy Spirit gets a hold of her—BOOM. I am telling you, one minute she is calmly preaching, the next minute you are questioning every life choice you have ever made while also feeling deeply loved. You do not ease into her sermons; you brace yourself. She does not yell; she does not scream. She detonates!

I love this church, but there was one thing that almost sent me back out the door. The church likes to hug. And I do not. I am not a hugger. I am a nodder. A wave-from-a-distance kind of girl.

So when I came the first time, I panicked! Because greeting at Emerge does not mean "hello." It means full body contact. At first, I handled it like a football game.

Dodge left.
Sidestep right.
Fake smile.
Quick escape.

I learned how to position myself behind people. I learned how to hold coffee like a shield. I learned how to look busy. And when all else failed? I threw Katy to the lions.

"Oh look! There she is! She loves hugs!"

Katy, being the saint she is, would just sigh and accept her fate. I am getting better though. Now I hug. Briefly. Like... we hug, but we both know it is on a timer.

No one at Emerge pretends to have it together. Nobody is flexing perfection. Nobody is hiding scars. We show up real. We worship real. We love real. And somehow, God meets us right there—in the mess, the laughter, the awkward hugs, and the TNT sermons. This place did not try to change me. It let God do it. Here I learned God forgives, so I can forgive others, too, including those who purposely hurt me.

And yeah... I still watch for incoming hugs.

But this?

This is home.

CHAPTER 23 - The Truth I Finally Saw

God is my Father. Jesus is my Savior. He lives in my heart, and He has never left me. Not once. Looking back now, I can see Him everywhere.

He was the woman who gave me the scarf when I was freezing and did not ask my name.
He was the man who gave me food when I was hungry and had nothing to offer in return.
He was the strangers who showed up at just the right moment, the mercy I did not deserve but desperately needed. He was fighting for me the entire time; I just did not see Him because I was always looking down.

Down at my shame.
Down at my fear.
Down at my pain.

I never thought to look up.

"The Lord will fight for you; you need only to be still." — Exodus 14:14

I was never invisible to God. He saw me on the streets. He saw me in addiction. He saw me when I ran, when I failed, when I lost everything again and again. He never stopped pursuing me. Not with condemnation but with grace.

CHAPTER 24 - If You Are Still Reading

If you made it this far, I do not believe that is an accident.

I believe God has been walking with you the same way He walked with me—quietly, patiently, waiting for the moment you finally look up.

Maybe your story does not look like mine. Maybe it does.
Maybe you have survived things you never talk about.
Maybe you have been strong for so long you do not remember how to rest.
Maybe you do not even know what you believe anymore—just that you are tired.

I was too.

And what changed everything for me was not cleaning myself up.
It was not fixing my past.
It was not earning anything.

It was surrender.

If you are ready—right now, wherever you are—to stop running, to stop carrying everything alone, you can pray this.

Not because the words are magic.
But because Jesus hears honest hearts.

Jesus,
I need You.

I admit that I cannot do this on my own.
I admit that I have made mistakes, followed the
wrong paths, and tried to survive without You.

I believe You are the Son of God.
I believe You died for my sins and rose again.
I believe You see me exactly as I am—and still love
me.

Please forgive me.
Come into my life.
Heal what I do not even know how to name.
Take what is broken and make something new.

I give You my past.
I give You my pain.
I give You my life.

I choose You.

Amen.

□

If you prayed that—even quietly—welcome home.

Nothing about your past disqualifies you.
Nothing you have survived was wasted.
And nothing ahead of you is too much for God.

I know.

Because if He can carry someone like me through all of this...

He can carry you too.

Made in the USA
Middletown, DE
07 March 2026

29142995R00060